CR
8.95

PS3569.L3

poems

David R. Slavitt

Louisiana State University Press *Baton Rouge* 1998

Designer: Michele Myatt Quinn
Typeface: AGaramond
Printer and binder: Thomson-Shore, Inc.

Library of Congress Cataloging-in-Publication Data

Slavitt, David R., 1935–
        PS3569.L3 : poems / David R. Slavitt.
          p.   cm.
        ISBN 0-8071-2300-5 (cloth : alk. paper). —ISBN 0-8071-2301-3
(pbk. : alk. paper)
        I. Title. II. Title: PS3569L3.
        PS3569.L3P7   1998
        811'.54—DC21

98-20570
CIP

The author is grateful to the editors of the following publications, in which some of the poems collected here previously appeared: *Edge City Review, Georgia Review, Janus, Light, Pequod, Poet's Voice, Poultry: A Magazine of Voice, Shenandoah,* and *World Poetry: An Anthology of Verse from Antiquity to Our Time* (W. W. Norton).

For Shoshana and Sam

Contents

1 Poems

Paradise Lost: An Alternative Version   1

Adam   2

Tryma   3

Invocation   5

Wonder Rabbi   6

Ghazal   7

The Second Murderer   8

As If   10

The Emperor's Rejoinder   12

Smart Remarks   13

Insomnia   14

Contents

L'Ennui de la Nuit   15

The Dead   16

Presbyopia   17

The Exigency of Rhyme   18

The Art of Translation   19

Posing   20

Cézanne Drawing   21

Northern Renaissance   22

Helen, Later   23

Whore   24

Off Tehuantepec   25

Beach   27

Paying the Piper   28

Rudiments   30

Desk Set   32

Just Desserts: A Life of Nesselrode   41

The Bear: An Epithalamion   47

Patriot   51

2 Translations, Imitations, and Caprices

The Vigil of Venus   59

Reading Pindar   65

A Garland for Meleager, the Gadarene Swain   68

Horace: Ode XXXVIII   73

Contents

Blueprint for Disaster, *by Christian Morgenstern*   74

Summons (*Die Behörde*), *by Christian Morgenstern*   75

Like a Loony   76

Broads: Jorie, Sharon, Lucie, and Louise   78

Bette Davis: The Tragic Muse   81

Remembering Marcello   82

Feet: An Anniversary Nonet   83

Domitian at Ostia   84

Recent Acquisitions   85

Bucolic Lines Composed en Route to Lyon's
U-Pik-'Em Strawberry Fields, Creedmore, N.C.   86

Niagara Falls   87

PS3569.L3   88

1

Poems

Paradise Lost: An Alternative Version

Of man's first disobedience and the fruit . . .
Now, there's a peachy pair. But this was an apple.
And how do you like them, keeping the doctors
away? Apples and oranges fill the philosophers'
baskets in which they never put all their eggs
or count chickens before they hatch or come home
to roost. Obey these rules or you're asking for trouble.
But it's fruit we were talking about, pears, Anjou
or Bosc, and nectarines, and pomegranates,
and those little bananas markets mostly don't have,
and greengage plums, or medlars, either unripe
or starting to rot, unless you're lucky. An ugly
fruit? Ah, no, the uglifruit is different.
It's a curse greengrocers learn to live with. (Gladstone's
father was a greengrocer, and although they say
the fruit never falls far from the tree, the son
rose, went into government, I do believe.)
But fruit, yes. It's the first commandment. The Lord
said unto Adam and Eve, "Be fruitful," and Adam
didn't crack wise as he well could have done: "Fruits!
Gardens! Leave me alone. What is this produce
production?" Man's first failure to find just the right
tart retort. (What tarte? What torte?) Raspberries
are what he should have delivered, or, no, at La Scala,
when the tenor is fat and the diva's tremolo wavers
all around the note except on it, they throw
the ripe fruit they have brought along with them in bags
from their gardens at home, to express profound displeasure.

Adam

Two Paradises 'twere in one
to live in Paradise alone.
—Andrew Marvell

So Adam is naming the creatures, the bull and the cow, and the ram and the
ewe, and the horse and the mare, and the rooster and the hen, and the drake
and the duck, and after a while he begins to understand the pattern of this
and he looks up and asks:
"What about me? The 'man' and the 'what'? How is it that only I do not have a
mate and that I am the only one for whom there is not a female of my kind?"
This is not a surprise to the Lord, who has already thought to Himself: "It is
not good for man to be alone," but He has done nothing about it, and the
rabbis wonder why not, what could He possibly be contemplating?
There is a long silence in the study house and perhaps a fly buzzes at the
window as the rabbis try to imagine what might have been in the divine
mind, which means that they have to imagine themselves as wiser, larger,
better, which is to say more generous, and at length the eldest of them,
stroking his yellowing beard, suggests:
"Let us suppose that the Almighty, blessed be He, hesitated because He
understood what was going to happen. He knew what Eve would do and
knew that Adam would complain to Him. So He waited until Adam asked
on his own, and only then, and with a heavy heart, He gave."
Now let us imagine the venerable rabbi getting up and opening the window so
the fly can escape. But it is late in the season, and the rabbi knows that there
is no escape and that the fly will die anyway.
Nobody says anything, because what is there to say?

Tryma

A tryma is a nutlike drupe.
No one in your playground is likely to respond
to such an observation in any reasonable way, but
you can always explain that a drupe has a single endocarp,
which is true but not, perhaps, helpful.

A pneuma is, by extension, a breathlike trope?
That, we may agree, would be horsing around, but
a drupelet, which is a small drupe, as, for example, the pulpy grain of the
    blackberry,
would have, logically, an endocarplet.
When it rains, as it may from time to time,
I can imagine you running through the meadow exclaiming,
"Ah, see the droplets on the druplets!"

You will be an exquisite child,
or, rather, are already but you will proclaim it
in such a way as to defy the world.
And will they call you on the carplet?
Defy them, defy them.

The trauma of the tryma
is with us always, as are the poor
in spirit, who will stare at you blankly
or in resentment ask,
"Wha'? Who?"
Answer them smartly and tell them
the wahoo is a kind of Euonymous
(which is a good name)
with arillate seeds.
Tell them your grandfather said so.

If that doesn't work, and it won't, you can take some comfort
from knowing that the false aril originates

from the orifice instead of the stalk of an ovule,
as in the mace of the nutmeg, which is an arillode.

It follows, I suppose, that a true aril is a false arillode,
although people seldom say so,
but never let that stop you.

Invocation

We are gathered here today in the presence of God and this company
to form a more perfect union, establish justice, ensure domestic tranquillity,
and provide for the common defense of the people, by the people, and for the
  people,
and we here do solemnly swear
to preserve and protect the Constitution of the United States of America
and the republic for which it stands,
forsaking all others, and deriving its just powers from the consent
of the huddled masses yearning to be free,
whose broad stripes and bright stars are indivisible,
and with liberty and justice for all.
It is for us the living rather to be dedicated here to the proposition
that all men are endowed by their Creator with certain unalienable Rights, and
that among these are the mountains, and the prairies and the oceans, white
  with foam at the twilight's last gleaming.
Do not send, therefore, to ask for whom the bell tolls;
ask, rather, what you can do for your country
to support this declaration with a firm reliance on the protection of Divine
  Providence.
We mutually pledge to each other
our Lives, our Fortunes, and our sacred Honor.
Let no man put asunder what God has joined together
to make his countenance to shine upon you
and give you peace. Amen.

Wonder Rabbi

for Deborah

So, nu?
What he knew! Ah, you
couldn't imagine, couldn't begin to begin
to imagine. To say he knew
the Talmud would miss the point. He knew it through
and through. But more than knew.
He was the book, had translated it to himself
and himself to it, to own it and be owned.
Listen, if you would open to any page
and let a straight pin touch on a word and then,
heaven forbid, push, so that it went through,
he knew, page after page, that sage,
that remarkable Jew,
what word your pin would pierce, would know, even feel
in his nerves the penetration of that steel
and he could explain to the men who stood around
in wonder what the words would be in order,
and give an interpretation that showed the real
meaning of their conjunction this way, reveal
the secrets that were hidden there, profound
and ancient mysteries, and make you, too,
for the moment at least rich in understanding.
Such, anyway, were the stories the old folks told
of what he could do,
that rabbi, when he was only seven years old.

Ghazal

With the rage and longing you'd see in a hurt child,
I challenge heaven with my plea—of a hurt child.

Is the rest of his life an afterthought, a footnote:
the psychopathology of the hurt child?

There is always that connection, an iron bond.
"Or leather, let it be," says the hurt child.

Others, more gently reared, may misconstrue,
but the world is harsh. "Trust me," says the hurt child.

But afterward, the remorse, on both sides, and the love
the others can scarcely imagine, and they envy the hurt child.

Think of David's love for his son, and Absalom's
for him. In that reciprocity is the hurt, child.

The Second Murderer

Clar. In God's name, what art thou?
2nd Mur. A man as you are.
Clar. But not, as I am, royal.
2 Mur. Nor you, as we are, loyal.
            —Shakespeare

People assume it's a rank. Second lieutenant?
Fiddler? Mate? Why not, therefore, a second
murderer . . . ? Plausible, but incorrect,
and the implications are misleading. There's no
exam I'd sit for to be promoted, no
august committee before which I'd have to appear
to get to be first murderer. That is a different
calling altogether. We are not like them,
not, if I may say, hotheaded, fanatic. . . . To be
neutral, let us call it *engagé*.
Your first murderer has a cause, an end
to justify his means. He cares, you see.
We are more balanced, reasonable people.
To us, it's a job, unpleasant perhaps, but jobs
often are. Your first murderer goes at it
with fervor in his heart, on principle.
We, less grandiose, are mostly after
profit, one way or another. Like most of you.
        Another misconception has us
second murderers not so much assistants
as bumblers, oafs—but if we were so inept,
why would they need us? And they do, indeed,
need our presence. Committed as he may be,
your first murderer's not an expert, requires
help, more often than not, to get the job done.
More important, a second murderer changes
him from an undistinguished killer and mere cutthroat
to a leader. Now, it's a project, an enterprise

with a mission statement, an organizational plan,
and all that fine administrative framework
to disguise, a little, the unattractive truth.
Why else risk taking a witness along?
It's not an excursion. Nobody ever says:
"I'm off to kill the Duke of Clarence. Join me?
And afterwards, perhaps a spot of supper . . . ?"
Nevertheless, there is a social dimension,
a need he has for complicity, to share
that burden of guilt he'd otherwise bear himself.
I think it's a kind of marriage—for each of us, knowing
the other's secret, can bring him down. Joined now,
made kin to us by that blood we have shed together,
he knows he's never absolutely alone.
A danger, it's also a comfort, or was once. . . .
Now, with your Oswalds and your Sirhan Sirhans,
it doesn't cross their minds to recruit one of us.
Why? My guess for what it's worth is that guilt
has spread so wide that no assassin worries
in the night's dark moments lest he be the worst man
alive in the world. He's crazy, but not enough
to feel cut off from mankind—not these days.
I'm semi-retired. But I still keep my beeper.

As If

God does not really mean the world literally.
    —Robert Musil

"And does the defendant have anything to say?"
As the judge peers down from the bench, the well-read villain
replies he didn't really mean it literally.
His honor, laughing, imposes, nevertheless,
a sentence the malefactor may, if he likes,
consider as metaphoric, those long years
a mere figure of speech, for what is time,
or space, or even, for that matter, matter?
The oncologist's pronouncement, however grave,
is also a semiotic gesture, a mordant
trope from which the patient abstracts himself,
the point of the conversation as likely as not
being the way the sunlight gleams on the doctor's
pen-stand, or how, with the prominent hairs of his eyebrows,
he resembles a huge bug. Flights of fancy?
Or glimpses of God's odd truth? It's a consolation,
Musil's notion that these are rhetorical figures
and the world is an analogue for something else,
an anodyne for the pain that may feel real
but that God cannot intend in a literal way,
unless Musil didn't mean "literally" literally.
Is the *New York Times* in code? In our search for meaning,
for clarity in this muddle, we suppose
the world may be a backdrop, an indication
of something going on elsewhere on the canvas
or beyond the frame where we are unable to see it.
There that tree that is painted falling falls
in the eerie silence philosophers frighten us with.
Does that improve our case or make it worse?
Never mind meaning; we settle gladly for pattern,
the tensions and resolutions of dance or music's

order of chords. For the reassurance of rhythm,
we invent a god to thank. The faint heartbeats
and the gentle up-and-down of my mother's breathing
as she held me at her breast . . . That's what I want,
literally, but can't ever have again
except by the mind's extension, despair's routine
contrivance, which, God knows, is worth the world.

The Emperor's Rejoinder

Nakedness is not, itself, the disaster,
but the moment of realization that, yet again,
I seem to have left my clothing somewhere . . . that's bad.
The cool aplomb in which I was somehow clad
deserts me. The truth of such dream scenes is exposed—
for the psyche, when it makes jokes, never strays far
from the literal. That others have had the identical
dream is cold comfort. The folktale relies
on this common nightmare, but omits, so as not to distress
small children, the obvious ending. The crowd's
laughter subsides at length, and no one takes notice
of how the emperor, furious, glares at the boy
who broke the spell and orders his household guards,
as I have done, myself, many times: "Kill him."

Smart Remarks

The attention of even the fondest parent wanders
while the babbling child utters epigrams, aperçus
La Rochefoucauld or Villiers de L'Isle-Adam
would envy. Or we forget, which is worse, those pearls

from the mouths of our own babes, cast before swine
(ourselves, that is). Thus, Alexandrias burn
all day, all night. In the desert, we try to imagine
despite our better judgment something better,

a God who is neither omnipotent nor omniscient
but at least can remember most of what He hears:
our sobs, our cries of joy, and the smart remarks
children sometimes make to parents—our prayers.

Insomnia

Between those LED numbers I can't read
without my glasses, a colon flashes, flashes
what once would have been ticks, its sickly green
representation that time continues to pass—
or accusation. To be awake at this hour
is punishment, which implies some guilt, bad habits

at the very least—those naps in the afternoon
for which this penance is now exacted: for flights
from the burden of consciousness, these random exiles
from sleep's homeland. No, that's too neat, too easy.

Figure a petty crook who works the borders.
Cops on both sides and customs inspectors know me,
put up with me, but now and then, for fun,
make me wait, sweat me, because they can.

L'Ennui de la Nuit

I can make out single words, a title or someone's
name, but never more than a phrase. . . .

         In dreams,
I am illiterate, analphabetic.

        Angry
or hurt at the loss, I learn to fake it, get by
on cunning or luck, but risk the mortification
of Latin class (another nightmare).

         A distant
child is sending desperate messages: Come
back!

    But I have lost touch with him, that tyrant-
king of the squalid island paradise
we all came from but never can return to,
although we may yearn for its hot sun, cool breeze,
and breakers hushing seabirds' cries.

         Oh, boring!
But God is boring, and happiness, most of the time.
Pain occupies the mind.

       I wake in a sweat
in one of panic's crevasses, another banal
example of *Liebestrauma.*

        But that's not it.
The child-king has sent a communiqué
scrawled on a paper he knows I cannot read—
that I am the castaway.

       His empty bottle,
lovely, green as the sea, has vanished, leaving
a precious tang of salt. And frangipani.

The Dead

The dead are absentminded,
                              miss birthdays,
anniversaries, holidays, great events,
neglect even to make excuses. . . .
                                   Distracted?
Otherwise occupied?
                     And yet they appear,
visit, vivid as ever, to offer
                         from time
to time—from timelessness to time—advice,
solace, or interest, when they feel somehow prompted.
Or simply company.
                        Their pressing engagements
take them off, away again.
                           And we
try to behave like the good children we were
and not vex with useless complaint.
                                   They know
that, after the pain subsides, the comfort stays.

And we forget that pain or even learn
the rudiments of their absentmindedness.

Presbyopia

Corrective lenses, assuming somehow that the eye
is erroneous, impose their errors, compound,
refract, to approximate exactitude. . . .
How can this be? At night, I squint to descry,
from the greenish blur I see in a black surround,
clear numbers, information, data, food

for the hungry mind, or anyway, left lobe.
The right delights in whatever there is, the softened
edges of things, as if of vague ideas
that might condescend to exist a while on the globe,
or maybe not. Those distant trees are often
a generalized green smudge that we see as

separate leaves because we think we know
better than what we perceive, and call that real.
My vision is fine if I hold the page to my face,
and the world deserves such scrutiny too, although
it's only the pope at airports and pilgrims who kneel
to kiss the ground and study a little space

as if it were a holy text. It is,
and its blurring is part of the lesson. Clarity
and truth are not the same. I try and fail
to feel at home in impressionist canvases
and the failure too is instructive, correcting me
in moral lessons of balance, tension, and scale.

The Exigency of Rhyme

It distracts the mind to allow
for an openness, somehow
holding a thought but not
being held by it or caught
in its implication as we
otherwise surely would be. . . .

Better yet, I remember a door-to-door Bible salesman who,
when business was bad, would offer the rubes he sold the Good Book to
his "autographed Bibles." "Signed by Jesus Christ? No way!"
"Of course not, lady! I signed them myself," the salesman would say,
"but look at that writing. It's plainly not my fist. I swear
on a stack of my own fine product that the Holy Spirit is there
guiding my hand when I do it." And the skeptical prospect pales,
as often as not, and the drummer writes up one more of his sales
of expensive Bibles with leatherette binding, a ribbon, and maps
of the Holy Land in the back—and a signature that perhaps
isn't quite his own. Which is what we poets can also claim,
though few of us go so far as to substitute for our name
the Lord of Hosts' or an angel's or one of those shoemaker's elves'
without whose help we could never have said such things ourselves.

The Art of Translation

Suppose that every tree translates
the wind into its idiolect, timbres
of differing timbers. Redolent now of pine pitch,

now of gum, or the duff of the oak grove,
it cleanses itself as fresh as when it arose
from the puffed-out cheeks of the ancient god.

In town, each gable and chimney modifies it
however slightly, enriching with commentary
and interpretation a never-changing text,

which is, however, without such impedimenta
mute and without such bodies unembodied.
Performance is, perforce, a misconstruction,

but better than none. As consonants drop away
the vowels will howl the same in your mouth or mine,
in a babe's or sage's: ooooh, eeeee, and aaaaah!

Posing

for James Albertson

A moue of concentration, which then explodes
into a rictus of effort . . . One might read them
as kisses and boyish grins
                              to beguile the muse?
or placate?
                    I have to try not to smile myself,
to hold the pose, and be a good subject.
                                              Time
passes, and I become, more and more, my body.
It is, like iris, goldfish, fruit, the light's
plaything,
                    an object in a world of other objects,
while his becomes his darting, devouring eyes.

Lower, somehow connected, behind the easel
a hand that has nothing to do with him or me
moves, pauses, and moves, its scratchy noises
the language of our exquisite conversation.

Cézanne Drawing

Distracted, angry, even disgusted, depressed . . .
In another time, you would have gone to church,
but now you repair to a nearby museum to pray
to the secular pictures for peace,
                                                    but cannot see,
blinded by turmoil. Nothing deigns to speak.
The paintings are silly daubs, palpable fakes,
increasing your unease until, in a corner
gallery, some of Armand Hammer's drawings
beguile you, unassertive gestures of ink
or chalk, so modest that much of the paper is bare.

In a sketch by Cézanne, a few nervous lines above
an indication of foreground greenery show
the shape of Mont Sainte-Victoire, its height, its distance,
a quick glance in fresh air. The world is the same,
no better than before, but you are healed,
rétabli, can stand it, at least for a while,
and you give thanks to abstract and distant gods.

Northern Renaissance

Rembrandt, Hals, and Vermeer
never went anywhere.
They liked it here.

Leave Holland? Why,
when it takes a lifetime to learn the sky
and study the lives of objects, dark or bright
according to their dialogue with the light?

Through travel what do we learn
but nostalgia—the reverse of the souvenir?
And yet any moment's vision will turn
into something else: we'll long for what was here
a moment ago and is gone, and therefore dear.

Hals and Vermeer
and Rembrandt at their easels tried to catch
such glints and glimpses as they could, to match
in patient strokes on canvases with paint
the stolid giddiness in what is near
at hand but delicate, growing faint,
and in an instant apt to disappear.

Helen, Later

In the city again, the palace and bed she belongs in,
but not in the bloom of her all-but-unbearable beauty
the years have stolen and no mighty armada,
having laid waste some Asiatic city,
can ever take back. Still, in a certain light,
Menelaus can look at Helen and sometimes see it,
or look and not see what he still remembers
of what she had been and try not to hate her for it.
Good manners can get them through the days, mostly; at night
they're on their own, clinging or turning abruptly
away in a disgust neither tries to hide.
Blame the gods as they may, their wounds and caresses,
flesh will claim for itself in the life it knows,
Menelaus' squalid kingdom, to which she's come home.

Whore

She had to have understood he'd picked her out
as a joke or for some other, odder, but just as unflattering
reason. Almost the eldest now in that *maison
close* and the ugliest (if that was what she had going,
it worked, was better than nothing, than being out
on the streets or under the bridges), she was accustomed
to being taken that way from behind, while his friends
watched, although very few kept on their hats
or kept their cigars in their mouths, as he did, puffing
and pumping, as if she were plumbing, as if she were meat.
It wasn't the first time, and she knew too well
the battery, spasm, the small warm spurt, and then
the abrupt withdrawal. Still one has to wonder
if she had some abstract sympathy for him, guessing
however dimly that this was the best he could do,
the closest he could come to what people mean
engaging in such an act. His rage and disgust
had nothing to do with her, except in this,
her divining what he might think or feel, or, worse,
her acceptance of it, submission to it—more
than he could bear. His name, Gustave Flaubert,
wouldn't have meant a thing to her. But she did
know him, and knew he'd think of her sometimes,
or dream. . . . What more can a girl expect in this life?

Off Tehuantepec

It may be a knack for being sensorially aware without having to
talk to themselves about what it is they are aware of that accounts
for the Indians' frequent long silences: if you do not talk to your-
self, you have less need to tell anyone else what you feel or think.
—Kelly Cherry, *Writing the World*

That steady snore astern and the prow's goose-vee
possess the sailors' ears with a conch-shell roar,
a focus of unremitting ambient sounds.

We are off Tehuantepec on that slopping sea,
bemused by its gentle motion. Or is it our breathing
and the pulse of our own vessels? Who can say?

But who can refrain from speech? Those souls on shore
the conquistadors thought they had mastered know the trick
of silence and, in their infant equipoise,

float on a surface, unmarked, unremarked,
an aspic shimmer of time. Do our furled sails
resemble umbrellas? Perhaps, but better not say.

Does the woodwork look like chocolate? *Taisez-vous.*
Ne bavardez pas! Content yourself with gazing,
as a cat can in its flawless attention. Let

recognition bloom, and then assent
may perfume the glade, at least for a while as the sun
climbs high in the bleached-out sky and the parrots' racket

subsides. We give ourselves over then to breathless
waiting for the random chirr of insects,
which stops, or does it? In the all-too-lively ear

it echoes still. What sense does that make? (I am going
a little mad perhaps—but call that sane,
the yammer under control, albeit barely,

and the thoughts of *Lustmord* merely that, though vivid.)
Walking is hard, those footfalls an invitation
for ravings to well up. How do the Toltecs

or whatever they are manage? Falling asleep
did they fend off serpents, jaguars, and outsized raptors
with the bouts of mathematics that made those millstone

calendars for grinding time to discrete
shards? But these are our guides to silence: they live
in a Godlike patience not even He could maintain,

whose word of beginning also implied an end.

Beach

These dull stones washed in the surf will shine
as we do too—as age and its cares sluice off
to leave huge toddlers taken unawares
in their awkward gambols, braving the waves this way

and then the undertow that. Staggering, leaping,
and then, letting go for a moment or two, they float,
allow themselves to be rocked and cradled as infants
in the arms of the sea that is truly, then, their mother.

But then the light changes; shadows lengthen; a cool
breeze kicks up to announce that the day is dying:
only the naughty dawdle, facing away
from the beach umbrellas and sand dunes to the water
where the blue-green turns a deeper blue to consider
how they might proceed correctly either way.

Paying the Piper

By the River Weser, wide and deep,
abandoned cemeteries keep
      the bones interred

of Hammel's grief-stricken dead—the poor
parents of 1484
      who waited for word

in the hope that their children yet might be
alive somewhere. Ignoring them, we
      read to our cheerful

issue a sanitized nursery rhyme
of what happened once upon a time.
      It is a fearful

tissue of lies—the end, I mean,
with Browning's semi-comic scene
      in Transylvania,

where all the little kids survive.
Safe and sound, they prosper and thrive
      away in Romania.

Pay the piper! Do it soon,
for later he may change his tune—
      I will not quarrel.

As far as it goes, it's probably true,
and what I tell my children, too,
      the poet's moral.

But after I have said "Good-night,
sleep tight, don't let the bedbugs bite,"
      I have to steel

my heart to how it really was,
for perverts don't keep moral laws,
        and evil is real.

Those body parts the townsfolk found
hanging in trees and strewn on the ground . . .
        Imagine the worst

and think then, what is there to say?
We shouldn't lie their griefs away,
        whose age is cursed

with Jeffrey Dahmers everywhere.
We turn to drink, perhaps to prayer,
        or just keep quiet,

shocked when a youngster whines and pesters
for a *Golden Book of Child Molesters.*
        But we won't buy it.

Rudiments

In a darkness that children fear,
she is turned to a child again
as if time could reverse itself
or, abandoning *now* and *then,*
just stop, having given up
on very old women and men.

Words, too, are blurred, but she keeps
a careful track of space:
the route from her chair to the kitchen,
the bathroom, her bedroom. Her face
is a map of the perils she gropes through
like furniture out of place.

In the afternoons, her daughter
comes to sit by her each day
for an hour. Their talk is awkward,
repetitive. . . . What they say
is beside the point, but her hand
on her daughter's knee that way

is soothing. She's waited for this
all day, and what agitates
or distresses her, though it remains,
at least for a while abates.
The daughter prepares her dinner,
feeds her, and washes the plates.

Then the ghosts return in their shifts
that are endless. The practical nurse
is frightened, but so is my aunt,
who may moan sometimes or curse,
or simply refuse to speak
in a rage that is even worse.

I think of them there, and weep,
and try not to rail against
how things turn out, and yet,
when I am depressed or tense,
at the end of my tether, I think
of those two and the rudiments

of courage and love in the mute
pressure and warmth of the touch
they exchange. It keeps them going.
It's what a life comes to, such
a gesture, a respite. O Lord,
how little it is, and how much.

Desk Set

1

By some trick of light or grace,
the forlorn commonplace,
abruptly enriched, will appear
to be waiting for its Vermeer

to demonstrate what we have not
ever completely forgot. . . .
Look at some desktop trinket
you've had for years; you may think it

lucky or charmed: it is much
deeper than that, for your touch
inheres, suggesting this
is what the whole universe is

or would have been, had you tamed it,
conquered it, somehow claimed it.
But after the flood or the fire
what remains of that empire

and its generations of men?
This paper knife, this pen,
or blotter or pencil cup,
to show that it wasn't made up.

2

The string of my worry beads
frayed, gave way. I had to have the beads
restrung—and have to worry now about the beads themselves,
which ought to have functioned as emblems
without assuming, without presuming. . . .

They impose themselves now as an independent subject
of worry: thirty-three beads and a marker bead.
They have some Islamic significance,
although I bought them in spite of that,
which is, I suppose, another reason to worry.
What does Islam know that the rest of us don't?
Are there only thirty-three worries? Are you hungry,
are you thirsty, are you cold, have you had a good bowel movement recently,
will you dream you are falling but, this time, not wake, actually hit, and die
    upon impact?
And so forth, for twenty-eight other categories of concern . . .
What sage or lunatic came to this abstruse reckoning? And was he
right? Was Spinoza right? Or Leibnitz? (That can't be a worry!)
There must be a miscellaneous category, which enables
but also defeats the entire system. What if
my jeweler calls, tells me the beads are restrung,
and I go and get them, only to find that I have nothing left to worry about,
    and have wasted my money
having had them restrung? I pray
for a life in which that could be a legitimate source of worry.
I cannot imagine such a life, but I am already vertiginous with envy
of the protagonist of my sudden fiction. . . .
The worry beads are blue and white, irregular, and nicely
nubbly to the touch. It is comforting to flick them with one's thumb.
That's an answer, albeit not a sufficient one. But what was the question?
Ah, yes, Leibnitz' first name—was Gottfried,
which is one less thing to worry about, except that I am likely to forget it,
which is deplorable but one of the consequences of getting older, and another,
    and slightly more serious subject for concern.

3

The print shows Harlequin, leaning, hovering over
recumbent Columbine. Behind him gauzy
curtains of tall French windows billow, looming
as Harlequin's outstretched wand swags them cloudlike.
On the ornate, pale blue chaise in the foreground, the girl

in ballerina's dancing slippers and tutu
appears to be sleeping—her dreams also cloudlike.
On the back, on the label age has foxed, I read
"Framed Specially for R. H. Macy & Co.,"
and below, in Palmer-method script, "Goodnight
Columbine" and then the name of the artist,
one "W. E. Webster." Nothing of interest,
except that my mother one afternoon must have paused,
must have been drawn to this once, her hand, her fancy,
hovering over that bin and lighting here.
Something I'm looking at now but cannot see
called out to something in her—the clown, the sleeping
girl, the open window, the wand, the curtains.

The title is odd. In the print, he is not leaving,
but coming in to wake her and turn her dream
sweetly, lovingly real. That upheld wand
is unambiguous, surely, as is the opened
window through which he has gained entry. Would mother
have known? Would she have needed or wanted the prudish
title? If she noted it, would she have thought it
mere good manners, or else seen through it? Ignored it?
It hung on the wall, in the hall as I remember,
above the Queen Anne bench. . . . Or was that a mirror?
The whole house has blurred. I dream of returning,
but the train breaks down, or the car, and I have to shift,
to improvise—I wade through thick muck, frightened,
exhausted. . . . These are nothing like Columbine's dreams,
whose name suggests the dove that betokens peace.

The scene is impossible: he is invisible; only
she can see him—or so the story goes—
which means that she has dreamt him, summoned him up,
wand and all. Hers is the magic, and he
is her sprite, an Ariel mostly but Caliban too,
and like them, almost tame. Most women think
we're something like that.

My father in that silly
suit? But forget the clothes, and note the longing,
that representation of Harlequin's tender gaze,
the love.
      I say her fingers, flipping through prints,
froze there in pleasure or recognition, and chose.

4

    In a line from an old screenplay,
    a man in a ship's café
    asks a sodden black-tied roué,
    "What does your wristwatch say?"
    who, after a moment's delay,
    replies in a deadpan way:
        "Ticktock, ticktock."

A joke, but not merely, for those iterated sounds are
consonants that give definition to time's howling vowels,
a ululation, a moaning the wind might make in its wildness
over the sea or the rolling expanses of desert, its drawn-out
primitive vocalise, necessary but hardly
sufficient for what we are proud to define as civilization.

Monks, soldiers, the men of routine hacked out their hours
of prayers and watches. The sailors, otherwise lost, demanded
a further precision by which to reckon their longitude—
therefore, chronometers, and all their heirs, our pocket watches,
wrist watches, atomic clocks, the microtome slicers
of time's not-quite-infinite sausage. The two timepieces

that adorn my desktop accuse me of wasting what they dole out,
never quite in synchronization. Perfect
devices with their quartz hearts would be cheaper than these complex
machines with springs, gears, escapements, balances, and such
paraphernalia as the industrial revolution adored. One,
an old silver Tavannes that hangs on its stand, I bought

on impulse during the three weeks or so I worked for Otto
Preminger, and tempus, it tells me, sure does fugit.
The other watch, a gift from my mother-in-law, an old-fashioned
railroad Elgin, used to belong to her father—who did
time. No one speaks of this, but from what I gather and guess,
some construction project went bad, the gouging and graft too much

for even gaudy and greedy San Francisco. My wife's
grandfather took the fall (isn't that what Jews were for?).
Cigars (I've got his gold matchbox too) and the good
high life of the inside deals made and unmade him—
this instrument ticked off moment by raffish moment. Its taint
remained, somehow, and, several years ago, when a thief,

athletic or desperate, climbed our roof to break in at my second-
story window, what he grabbed from the desk was only this watch.
Distressed by the loss of a kind of heirloom, I never told
my mother-in-law what had happened, but six months later, I heard
the major crimes division was having an exposition
of stolen property they had recovered and I went down,

despite the impossibly long odds, to look—to avoid
the guilt of not having tried. Among yards of watches, cameras,
bracelets, rings, gold chains, and other tawdry valuta,
loot from the war that never lets up between rich and poor,
or poor and poorer, I took my turn with the rest of the victims,
avoiding one another's eyes, ashamed of ourselves

as unlucky ones, the fools who could neither accept nor let go.
In hell, I imagine, processions of damned souls search like this
for what they had taken for granted, like health, like air, until
they lost it—virtue, innocence, faith, and love, the key
to the garden, the childhood toy, the token, the icon. The odds
are long. . . . But there it was, my watch! Two years went by

until, just before trial, the fence's lawyer worked out
a deal, and copped a plea. The policemen could then give back

the watch they'd held in their evidence safe, that jail for objects
from which only luck had contrived a way to spring it. It keeps
good time (but what other kind is there?) as each
day unwinds and we watch each other's running down.

5

The green bronze cat is Ptolemaic. A god . . .
I used to know of what, but for me, it means
folly and how, on rare occasions, with luck,
it may be forgiven, even rewarded. I bought it
twenty years ago, in a shop in Cairo . . .
having no idea that shopkeepers there could report
such sales, turn in their customers, get a reward
from the government. Smuggling such antiques affronts
the nation and, of course, is against the law.
I'd bargained, perhaps too hard, but he had approved.
It's the ones who agree too soon for whom his contempt
must prompt dropping the dime, or whatever coin
informants use there. Later, out at the airport,
with my cat stashed in a suitcase, I was too nervous
to wonder why the porter was so insistent,
and, not having spent quite all my Egyptian money,
gave him a pound—worth seventy cents or so—
to deal with the bags. He accepted the limp bill
and chalked a mark on my luggage: I had cleared customs.
The pound, of course, was right. To have given nothing
would have been provoking; giving more, if I'd thought to,
would surely have aroused suspicion. A pound
was exquisitely calibrated baksheesh. Not
by sophistication, or any *savoir vivre,*
but only by grace had I been saved. Cold sweat
prickled my back in the transit lounge as I waited,
thinking of what could have happened, of what could still
happen. Then the plane boarded, taxied, took off. . . .
I waited to hear the landing gear retract,
signaling I was safe. . . .

But the cat god reminds me
I was lucky that time, and no one is ever safe.

6

There are many pens,
as if each one
had its own voice
and I could make
a considered choice
among them, but
whichever I take
I grope and stammer,
forget how to spell
and even my grammar.
But still they beckon,
gleaming gold,
silver, and black,
some new, some old,
inviting my hand
to remove the cap
of one of them and
venture once more
a word, a phrase.
Sometimes it works,
and I forget
myself and become
a child again,
or an inert accessory
of the pen.

One is, in fact, solid gold,
the kind of pen that diplomats
use to sign treaties. . . . I like it
because it works as a touchstone does

but in reverse. If I know while I'm writing
with it that, yes, this is gold, expensive . . .
the words are probably worthless. But
if the pen disappears, turns into a plastic
Papermate or a Bic, then what
I am writing may not be without value.
One is my father's ancient Duofold,
green—it looked like malachite once.
Its cap still does, but the pen converts,
the nub at the end comes off, and instead
of a pocket fountain pen, it can serve
with its tapered quill in a stand, and did
for years on the desk in my father's office.
Years of sweat and sunlight faded
the green to a pale, ghost color, a ghost's
hand has never quite let go of.
I use it but only rarely, pretending
to be a grown-up, trying to pass
myself off as reliable, wise. . . .
I am intimidated by it,
used it to write the checks for my children's
tuitions. I used it to sign my will.

7

Other toys and baubles: a lapis lazuli
water buffalo, not Yeats' scholar's mountain
but not bad—a cow and her calf, and her horns
must have been hell to carve; a small Santa Clara
bowl, its lustrous black the result of the burning
horseshit they use, because wood is scarce, to fire
their almost useless pottery (water would melt it);
a peacock in cloissoné; a pretty inlaid
wooden stamp dispenser; an almost worthless
pocketknife I found years ago in the driveway
of the Cape Cod house—which is all I have left of it now;
a cheap dagger—its blade's braggart inscription:

"Never draw me without reason nor sheath me
without honor." I worry about that "nor."
A couple of goose-quill pens in a shot-filled holder.
A calculator. A magnifying glass.
They all hold their breath, attend, waiting with patience
that only objects know, who are sure they'll outlast
my whims and tastes, my history. Then, set free,
they will skitter away, dispersing to heirs, antique stores,
or trash heaps as would any flock of pigeons
after the bread crumb scatterer has gone.

Just Desserts: A Life of Nesselrode

1

What were the causes of the war
and what were the powers fighting for?
The Don Pacifico affair,
and the high French tariffs, yes, and there
were Nikolai's religious quirks
and his concern that, under Turks,
the Orthodox peoples were mistreated—
about which he could grow quite heated.

Oh, yes, all that, but there was also the underlying question we must steel
    ourselves to ask:
What's for dessert?

2

War is one thing, but a good cup of coffee and a great piece of pie . . .
Or pâtisserie? Would you prefair
a tarte from the carte? A small éclair?
A floating island? *Peut-être,* one
of these, a nice napoleon?

3

"Napoléon III was not a free agent. He was reined in by the institutions,
    customs, and legal practices that he inherited from his predecessors, and
    especially from his uncle. [Ah, mon oncle!]
It was hard to distinguish between authentic and sham, between what was
    genuine and what was imitation:
for this reason Napoléon III aroused more unmeasured slander from contem-
    poraries than any political leader since the days of Louis XVI. . . .
Yet, at the same time, Napoléon III undertook a vast program for the reform of

French institutions in the hope of giving the French people a richer life than any previously known in the history of the world.

More jobs, longer holidays, shorter hours, higher wages—these were the things he advocated and worked for.

He made Paris what it is—as far as appearance is concerned—the Paris of the great boulevards and the Paris of the operas."[1]

Also, he was fond of mille-feuilles.

4

Monsieur Mouy, chef to the Comte de Nesselrode, invented the pouding that bears his master's name:

A litre of custard sauce, 250 grams of chestnut purée, 125 grams each of candied orange peel and crystallized cherries cut in dice and soaked in Malaga; 125 grams of currants and sultanas, picked over, set to swell in warm water and then soaked in Malaga.

Add to this custard an equal amount of whipped cream flavored with maraschino.

Put this mixture in a large charlotte mold with a lid, having lined the base and sides with white paper. Close the mold and, to seal it hermetically, fill the lid opening with butter. Put the mold in ice and salt to set.

Turn out the pudding onto a serving dish. Take off the paper covering it and surround the base with *marrons glacés*.

Et voilà!

5

From Vladimir Kochubei's foreign ministry memorandum of 1829: "The advantages of the preservation of the Ottoman empire exceed the inconvenience which it presents."

This is the cornerstone of Russia's Turkish policy for a decade or more.

In 1833, the treaty of Unkiar Skelessi committed each to assist the other in case of war; a secret article exempted Turkey from having to furnish armed support to Russia on condition that it close the Bosphorus to foreign warships.

The Turks are also adept *confiseurs* and *pâtissiers*.

1. David Wetzel, *The Crimean War: A Diplomatic History* (Boulder, Colo., 1985), 22.

6

The soil between the Mamelon and the Malakoff could be cut like cheese.
Like cheese, sir. (Have a bit of Gouda? It's a Gouda cheese.)
MacMahon, whose division was to attack the Malakoff,
learned that the Russki troops were relieved invariably at noon,
the old ones moving out and then the new ones moving in.
He struck, therefore, at twelve o'clock precisely.
Cannon here and here, like these walnuts. (Have a walnut?
They go well with the cheese.) Decaen's men here, and Vinoy's men here,
with De Wimpffen's brigade in reserve and two battalions of Zouaves . . .
Anyway, there we are, and MacMahon carries the day,
all in white gloves if you please, as if at St. Cyr on parade,
and the Zouaves plant the flag, and the general says those famous words:
"J'y suis et j'y reste."

I am Swiss and I am tired, what? Have a pastry?

7

Had Tsar Nikolai relaxed just a little,
and had he referred to Napoléon III with the honorific *Mon Frère*
instead of the grudging *Mon Ami,* it all might have been otherwise.
L'Empereur replied with grace, "One inherits one's brothers, but one picks one's
    friends."
But, for dessert, *la guerre.*

8

Nesselrode, a German, born in Portugal,
served under five tsars. He was detested
by the xenophobes who called him "cosmopolitan."
He was. "To live in peace," he said, "that was the ideal;
and to achieve it, one must make reciprocal concessions and sacrifices,
and not demand the impossible."[2]

2. Nesselrode, *Autobiographie,* (Paris, 1904), 21–22.

43

The pouding can be used as a pie filling.

9

His father, Catherine's emissary to Lisbon,
opposed the young man's decision to be a diplomatist:
"He does not have the necessary qualifications. He does not have the devil
      in him,
and without the devil a diplomat will go nowhere."
But even the devil has his food.

10

His real opponent was Menshikov, Minister of the Navy.
He wanted the confrontation, he wanted the war.
Nesselrode thought it was nuts.
                              Cannon here, cannon here . . .
Menshikov's heirs fled to France and in Chartres set up
as *chocolatiers,* making elegant light-green dainties,
pistache pastiches, dusted lightly with sugar.

11

And what was it that a Crimean wore?
A cardigan. With raglan sleeves, no doubt.
And on his head, we may assume, a balaclava.

12

Tolstoy writes: "Along the whole line of the Sebastopol bastions—which for so
many months had been seething with such extraordinary life and energy, for so
many months had seen heroes relieved by death as they fell one after another,
and for so many months had aroused the fear, the hatred, and at last the admi-
ration of the enemy—no one was now to be seen: all was dead, ghastly, terrible.
But it was not silent: destruction was still going on. Everywhere on the ground,
blasted and strewn about by fresh explosions, lay shattered gun carriages crush-
ing the corpses of foes and Russians alike, cast-iron cannons thrown with ter-

rific force into holes and half-buried in the earth and silenced for ever, bombs,
cannon-balls and more dead bodies; then holes and splintered beams of what
had been bomb-proofs, and again silent corpses in grey or blue uniforms. All
this still shuddered again and again, and was lit up by the lurid flames of the
explosions that continued to shake the air."

A bombe: two or more layers of variously flavored ice cream in a round
or melon-shaped mold.

13

A gourmet, of course, but also a horticulturalist,
who had great success with his camellias, rhododendrons,
and azaleas. He traveled widely, took the waters
at all the fashionable spas, and loved the opera,
met Rossini at Troppau. He believed:
"socialism, communism, the disordering passion for democratic institutions,
the insane idea of reconstituting the public law
on imaginary principles of race, language, and nationality
[are] dangerous heresies against the unity and harmony of the natural order."

And Rossini—what did he believe? *Ma foi!* Or say, *ma foie,*
sautéed in butter with thick slices of truffle—
thus, tournedos Rossini.

14

There were also practical reasons for Nesselrode's caution.
The Russian ships in Sebastopol were "filthy, old fashioned,
badly maintained," said one report, "and impressive
only in the scale of their corruption."
Of thirteen vessels fitted for sea duty, six at most
were seaworthy; the rest were crippled by dry rot.

A nef is a golden vessel, shaped like a ship,
with cutlery, napery, salt cellars, and all such equipment,
used at the royal table. Even princesses,
passing the royal nef, had to salute it.

15

The army, sent out for a summer campaign on the Danube,
had nothing to do, the Russkis having retired.
(Is the war over already?) To teach them a salutary
lesson, Sebastopol! A siege in the Crimea
required however rather different equipment.

Baked Alaska? Very good, messieurs.

16

Generals January and February,
Nikolai said, would deal with the allied armies.
They dealt with him, too, chilled reviewing the troops.
Pneumonia, pleurisy, death. The proof of the pouding.
Alexander II succeeded. *Slava! Slava!*

17

La Gloire was what Napoléon wanted, the name
condemning him to it, but all his Crimean pigeons
came home to roost at Sedan, with MacMahon again,
now Marshal of course, and De Wimpffen and Zouaves,
but Ducrot had it right: "We are," he said, "at the bottom
of a chamberpot, *et nous y serons emmerdés.*"

The Bear: An Epithalamion

1

North of Montpelier, on the County Road, somewhere
beyond Bliss pond on the way to Calais, there
it was, crossing the road. . . . A dog? A bear!
At that size, with that peculiar lope, it was,
indeed, a young black bear! The city has
its thrills and dangers, but out here in the back
of beyond, there are also moments when the slack
nerves snap taut. A creature like that is rare
in a life like mine. An omen, then, a sign?
But we resist such notions as fate, benign
or otherwise. Still, my breath was different, my pulse
a bit faster. Perhaps it was somebody else
the spirits of the woods were speaking to,
while also showing off to an urban Jew
for whom such beasts are exotic, even bizarre,
as he drives along in his air-conditioned car
to a classmate's daughter's wedding. Her mother's Swiss,
from Bern, in fact, and one could suppose that this
is thus, their emblem. At least as a conceit
it seems an attractive notion one might propose
to amuse the bridal couple, or some of those
fond friends who will have assembled, some from great
distances, to approve and celebrate
the occasion. One need not, of course, allude
especially to the animal's negritude—
which is not irrelevant, but it would show a lack
of manners to mention that the groom is black.
A Haitian Seventh-Day Adventist, he;
a tiny thing, half-Swiss, half-Jewish, she.
Will John Peale Bishop's famous line resound
in other minds than mine? Can there be found
that ceremony by which somehow to unite

the huge Moor with Desdemona? Quite
a poem that was, and not at all about race,
or surely not only that. In this strange place
in Vermont, on these dirt roads in the woods, one may
wish Mariza and Dièry well, and say
"Happiness!" and "Long life!" and hope they fare
as well as any couple, while worried that they
may have a tougher row to hoe. They face
I cannot imagine what, or do not dare.
How does that shaggy animal betoken
anything good? Our fears remain unspoken.
None of us wants to be rude or even unkind,
and yet, there it is, for none of us is blind.
Perhaps they'll be all right, surviving, at length,
as the bear does close to town, on cunning, strength,
and luck, in whatever combination these
occur, as he preys on the local farmers' bees.

2

I might have forgotten it all, but that night very
vivid dreams possessed me. I'd driven back
to the motel on those dirt roads, winding, scary
with patches of fog. I'd prayed for lights and hard
paved surfaces, peering into the endless black
canyon my headlights picked out between the trees.
I came, at last, to a road that at least was tarred
on which I could stop to ask someone the way.
No great adventure, it was nonetheless upsetting:
one hates to admit his vulnerabilities.
Also sleeping alone in a strange place may
have had something to do with my dream—in which I lay
down in a bed with that bear, which cradled me
in its arms in a loving way I could not trust,
for I knew it feared and distrusted me. Our fear
was balanced against our love. I am forgetting
details, perhaps, but the situation was clear,

poignant, appealing. I lay there with it, just
barely breathing and feeling its hot breath on
my cheek. Together, grateful, terrified, we
held one another. It wasn't sexual. Huddled
together that way, different and yet with a brief
truce that obtained between us, we were cuddled
intimates. Waking up, I felt relief
at having survived what we had undergone
together, and gratitude, and also grief
for what that bear must bear, a shaggy beast,
lumbering, lonely, hot, and insect-ridden,
hungry for berries or fish or whatever feast
it can steal from the Vermonters' compost piles,
with the dangers everywhere in those woods, hidden
the night before behind each tree for miles.

3

A splendid wedding—a singing of hymns and psalms
to soothe the troubled beast. In the Old West Church,
the couple vow to love and trust each other,
as all couples do. The architecture calms.
The wind outside in the branches of maple and birch
soughs an assent. Their happiness seems rather
plausible, for the moment. But moments are all
we have. I think again of Othello and how
he knew there were risks, and Desdemona, too,
was willing to take a very long-odds gamble.
Our lives, otherwise, are cautious, mean, and small.
What's safe and easy doesn't require a vow
of what you solemnly undertake to do
before God and this company. The simple
ceremony is done, but will it hold?
We hope. The only other choice is despair
the killing in Port-au-Prince and Mogadishu,
Kigali, and Sarajevo have made the issue
of our decade: hate, generations old,

is stacking spindly corpses everywhere.
And yet, I woke, alive and well. My bear
and I held still for one another. These two,
each knowing what the other is thinking, may do
as well from moment to moment and day to day,
may thrive and prosper. I think of that animal's lope
across the field, and what I dare not hope
I can perhaps imagine and even pray.

Patriot

1

James V. Forrestal
responded to his country's call
(although the salary was small).
He read the writing on the wall.
"The Communists will kill us all,"
said Secretary Forrestal.

2

Why did Truman sack him? Was it,
as the first secretary of defense firmly believed,
a conspiracy of Jews and Communists out to get him?
Or might HST have been PO'd about JVF's contributions
to the Dewey campaign?
"Dewey? Who he?"
Go, know.

3

Commies, commies, commies,
coming up out of the toilet bowl,
ready to bite you in the tush,
sneaking out from the baseboards like little cockroaches
whenever you turn off the light,
invading the sacred precincts of our shores.
Yes, bugging the beaches, even at Hobe Sound.

Look, look, all those little holes. . . . You think they're for beach umbrellas?
Not so. Not so. Listening devices!
They are monitoring every word we say.
Especially those I say.

In a way, it was flattering,
but he did not give in to such blandishments.

Here the secretary of defense kneels down on the beach and pours
handfuls of sand into those holes set in the small concrete slabs.

4

From the Forrestal Diaries:
25 April 1947
Lunch at the Pentagon Building today with Judge Patterson, General
Eisenhower, General Spaatz, Admiral Nimitz.

(Or men who looked much like them.)

Admiral Nimitz expressed the view that Italy was a country of great
importance to the United States. . . . (It is only the existence of Italy that keeps
Switzerland from having a seacoast and being a great naval power.)

I said it was manifest that American diplomatic planning of the peace was far
below the quality of the planning that went into the conduct of the war.
We regarded the war, broadly speaking, as a ball game that we had to finish
    as quickly as possible.

Not a profound plan, perhaps, but a good plan.

5

It wasn't just ambition and it wasn't only greed.
He worked his little ass off when he worked for Dillon Read,
and they spoke of him with reverence over brandy and cigars,
for he was the one who fixed it so that Chrysler bought Dodge Cars.

6

Little Russian agents
have bugged the building, literally, with trained insects
under the watercress leaves on his sandwich plate
or crawling up and down along the radiator pipes,
reporting back not only his conversations
but unspoken thoughts that are sensitive, classified, secret, top secret.

They are cracking the code.
In desperation, one learns to write in plain cipher:

NOWIS THETI MEFOR ALLGO ODMEN TOCOM ETOTH EAIDO FTHEP ARTY.

7

James James Forrestal Forrestal Weatherbee George Dupree
took great care of his mother,
though he only was five foot three.
When he was at Dillon Read, and his father died,
he rented and furnished an apartment in Manhattan for his mother.
She never set foot in it.

8

Actually, he was five four,
one of those little guys. At Princeton
one of his nicknames was "Runt."
He took up boxing.
He got his nose broken when he hit the pro too hard at the athletic club.
It gave him a raffish look, accessorizing
the Brooks Bros. suits and the Peale shoes.

9

From the Forrestal Diaries:
19 July 1948
As to the question of who should get the bomb?
"It seemed to me that this might be settled by:
1. Assigning the atomic bomb to the Air Force on the basis of dominant
   interest.
2. Limiting Naval Air use of it to (a) sorties upon strategic targets at the
   direction of the Air Force; (b) sorties upon purely naval targets.
3. Accept a principal of 'dominant interest' with right of appeal by the Navy,
   first to the Joint Chiefs of Staff and to the Secretary of Defense."

We must all be good children and learn to share our toys.

10

A small but not insignificant sign of stress:
When nervous he would scratch at the bald spot on his crown.
He'd scratched it raw, bloody,
as if there were something in the brainpan he was out to get
that was out to get him.

11

James V. Forrestal
never liked to bathe at all,
but every hour on the hour,
took a shower.

12

The diagnosis: Involutional Melancholia.
This doesn't exist anymore.
The secretary is nevertheless still dead.

13

I am a camera.
I am the way and the truth and the life.
I am the grass. Today, I am a fountain pen.
I'm a pepper, you're a pepper, he's a pepper, she's a pepper. . . .
I'm a little teapot, short and stout.
I am an aircraft carrier.

Whatever you say, Mr. Forrestal.

14

From the Forrestal Diaries:
28 April 1947
"The Russians are planning to take over the whole world.
Look at Poland, Hungary, Czechoslovakia, Rumania, Bulgaria. . . . "

But we agreed to all that at Yalta. That was the deal.
That's what they won in the war. Remember the war?

"Still, it's a threat, a conspiracy, a plot. . . . Look at the fringe countries:
    Belgium, France, Denmark, Norway, Sweden. Communists can infiltrate
    into all of them."

Like the Buddhists in Ireland.

"Are you sure there aren't any?"

15

His intention was to hang himself.
Having tied the belt of his robe to the window sill,
he climbed out of the window, whereupon
the belt gave way.
The death was due, then, to the fall
from a sixteenth-floor window of the Bethesda Naval Hospital,
and the suicide—by defenestration—never happened.
The insurance company wasn't exactly cheerful,
but they paid the ten grand.

16

How then do we sum up the achievements of this man?
He was a raving loony, but not stupid.
He was the father of the Cold War
(although if we'd taken out those twenty Soviet cities when we had the chance,
as Forrestal wanted to do, there wouldn't have been a Cold War).

One of those little guys who box,
he was what the nation needed, or, say, deserved.

2

Translations, Imitations, and Caprices

The Vigil of Venus

I

Tomorrow love shall have its way with ingenue and old roué.
Spring has sprung, young, and singing rebirth,
inveigling lovers, as birds overhead mate and the trees
undo themselves and yield like maidens out on the field.
                                                    O Goddess!
Tomorrow love shall have its way with ingenue and old roué.

II

Orange blossoms and myrtle sprays: everywhere are brides' bouquets.
The world turns matchmaker and the woods are alive with whispers
like the giggles of young girls who are minions of Dione, nymph
and mother of Venus, queen of the green season's demesne.
                                                    O Goddess!
Tomorrow love shall have its way with ingenue and old roué.

III

Tomorrow air, water, and fire will all commingle in desire
as Dione, who arose like foam from the deep green sea,
teaches the world to primp, bedeck, sashay,
as wavelets caress with a loving hand the flank of the strand.
                                                    O Goddess!
Tomorrow love shall dictate to the old roué and the ingenue.

IV

Buds on all the plants and bushes display in vegetative blushes
a lust for life, as nature is all turned turgid,
tumescent, lubricated, with drops of morning dew
to dazzle at early dawn the inviting resplendent lawn.
                                                    O Goddess!
Tomorrow love shall have its way with ingenue and old roué.

V

This is the season when flowers cavort, sway in the wind,
in a dance of desire, their fronts damp with the juices of love
as if in the woods there were beds of the glands of Bartholin
with the tall fronds of night-blooming prostates viscid and white.
                                                      O Goddess!
Tomorrow love shall give free play to shy ingenue and old roué.

VI

Look at those petals, soft, inviting, the maidenly pinks
or matronly vermilions. The garden, lewdness run riot,
is the goddess' fantasy, lovely labia everywhere parting
and disclosing delicate features of the parts that enable our futures.
                                                      O Goddess!
Tomorrow shall love give salute to old campaigner and raw recruit.

VII

Stare at one of those gorgeous blossoms, really look hard,
and see how the plant's purpose, its telos, is this
putting forth of a sexual declaration of love,
a reaching out to wed the world and take it to bed.
                                                      O Goddess!
Tomorrow love shall have its way with ingenue and old roué.

VIII

Like a headmistress, the goddess declares a free day and sends
the girls to the woods in bevies to prowl the thickets and glades,
and with them a naked boy, a rogue with a quiver and bow
who shoots into the air barbs that land who knows where. . . .
                                                      O Goddess!
Tomorrow love shall come to the aid of old roué and blushing maid.

IX

But today is a holiday, so today he is quite disarmed,
lays his weapons aside, but nevertheless is a danger—
by that tiny pouch and button, who knows who may be smitten?
The girls are taking chances as they steal their furtive glances.

                                           O Goddess!
Tomorrow love shall have its way with ingenue and old roué.

X (XII)

Ceres and Bacchus attend the feast. There is much eating and drinking,
and the rhapsodist strums his lyre and sings what is in our hearts,
his vision Apollo's gift that he passes on to us all.
The woods resound with his songs and nightingales' all night long.

                                           O Goddess!
Tomorrow love shall have its way with ingenue and old roué.

XI

His sister, the goddess Diana, puts by her weapons and thinks,
reappraises her fate—for even a virgin may wonder
what she has lost as each sunset bids the world go to bed
and again as each moonrise discovers the intricate postures of lovers. . . .

                                           O Goddess!
Tomorrow love shall ride roughshod over the hearts of mortal and god.

XII (X)

At the least, for Venus' sake, Diana elects to take a respite
from her pursuit and slaughter of bird and scampering beast.
In this mood, the wood is transformed, and we glimpse a moment of peace,
no bloodshed staining the grass where shepherd lies down with his lass.

                                           O Goddess!
Tomorrow love shall have its way with ingenue and old roué.

XIII

On the heights of flowery Hybla, the goddess presides, declaring
freedom, ease, and rapture, but having lived long with constraint,
we do our best as stiff-jointed and heavy-footed we dance
to the pipe's seductive strain and gambol on Enna's plain.

O Goddess!

Tomorrow love shall have its way with ingenue and old roué.

XIV

All the girls of the village, the surrounding farms, and the hillside
pastures attend the summons of Cupid's mother, voluptuous
Venus, whose whispered dictates fill them with apprehension:
they're afraid to fail as indeed they are also afraid to succeed.

O Goddess!

Tomorrow love shall lie in wait for ingenue and sophisticate.

XV

They blush to hear her sing the praise of the god, her father,
who rains his fertility down from the sky to the lap of the fields,
and they feel in their own laps a shiver of sudden response,
an opening up of the truth of their powerfully fecund youth.

O Goddess!

Tomorrow love shall have its way with ingenue and old roué.

XVI

Her mystery is the power that kindles life from unlikely
opposites that encounter each other: Trojans and Latins
were joined when Aeneas bedded Lavinia; Romulus' sons,
in their lust for those Sabine women, blurred what it meant to be Roman.

O Goddess!

Tomorrow love shall have its way with native and with emigré.

XVII (XVIII)

By Venus' command did Mars, her former lover, attend
on Ilia, the Vestal virgin, forced her, and she brought forth
Romulus, Remus, Rome, Caesar. Civilization
and all the good things that it brings come from these passionate springs.
>   O Goddess!
Tomorrow love shall have its way with virgin and with débauché.

XVIII (XVII)

The tide of the huge future begins with these tiny spurts.
The scrotal tingle, the sudden vaginal lubrication,
are parts of the general lusts of the world at large. In the fields
the perfume of fresh-turned earth is the tang of their giving birth.
>   O Goddess!
Tomorrow love shall have its way with ingenue and old roué.

XIX

Venus arouses the woods, the meadows and fields. The hillsides
heave and the hidden valleys open in invitation.
Her son is a country boy whom she nursed at her beautiful bosom
into which he was tucked, clutching, rapt, as he sucked.
>   O Goddess!
Tomorrow love shall have its way with ingenue and old roué.

XX

Look how the mighty bull, the ram, and the spirited stallion
lie down in their pastures, content to feel the good warmth of the earth
as if it were an enormous cow or ewe or mare—
with something of mate and mother, a reliably welcoming other.
>   O Goddess!
Tomorrow love shall be high priest to every fish and bird and beast.

XXI

High in the sky the trumpeter swans perseverate swan-ness.
And smaller birds in the copse chirrup and coo—even Procne
and Philomel, the victims of Tereus' terrible lust.
The tunes in which they complain sound much like a lovesong's refrain.
O Goddess!
Tomorrow love shall preach its truth to every maiden, every youth.

XXII

They sing, but we are mute, dumbstruck with longing and hope
that spring may come to us, too, and our hearts burst into birdsong,
an anthem of celebration, creation, and re-creation.
Hatred is silent, and death. Singing requires breath.
O Goddess!
Tomorrow love shall have its way with ingenue and old roué.

Reading Pindar

1

Boasts, threats, lamentation, prophecies, prayers . . .
such authoritative speech requires more
than a clearing of the throat or sharp rap on the goblet's
rim.
     These words are acts,
                          or not acts, but real
things, no mean tricks or tricks of meaning:
facts, unblurred by hope and nostalgia, fixed.
We try to speak with justice,
                     say what just is,
but such clarity costs, is sharper than any
sword or Gurkha knife with metal thirsty
for honor and someone's blood, theirs, yours,
or even my own—it seems to make no difference.

The strong wine in the crater is not at all sweet:
the soft-spoken songs are, themselves, as they set their seal on
the athletes' victories, a great achievement.

2

Olympia 1

Hieron of Syracuse has won some horse race.
What's that to you or me?
                    "How about them Redskins"—
or Cowboys or Buccaneers? These children's names
emblazoned on the teams' helmets should not
confuse us, for living and dying is serious business,
and any victory quickens even the hardest
hearts. The stadium's roar is of praise and prayer
for redemption, nothing less. Their *aethlos* figures

any ordeal, and we, who hold our breaths
and then, when we breathe again, cry out as one
in triumph, know this.
                              In Hieron's feat and Pelops',
we can glimpse the prize of eternal life, that glory
that ought never to fade. Old-timers know
the score—that all the games are funeral games.

3

Olympia 14

He invokes the Graces, the queens of song, the queens
of Orchomenos—Aglaia, Euphrosyne,
and Thalia.
                    That theater closed long ago, I'm afraid.
But the show goes on. Through the Graces is all delight
for men and even the gods. Who has not seen
the shortstop's efficient throw to first where the runner
is always out by a step?
                                    What this affirms,
though none of us can explain it precisely, Echo
shall declare aloud at the base of the black wall
of Persephone's house, calling to Kleodamas
of his son's triumph. Asopichos won in the dash,
and now on his young hair, that wreath of glory
will shine for what he achieved in the games

                                                              and did

somehow for us.
                    But was it?
                                        Somehow, yes.

4

Nemea 6

Our ship pitches and yaws, and sensible Pindar
lets us know that the only waves to fear

in the whole wide ocean are those approaching the keel.
How else to impress or amaze our dopiness
except with what's at hand? The athlete's speed
is there for us to see in the stadium. Then
he lopes on his victory lap.

                       There is no Hector
he has to drag in the dirt, for we will grant him
splendor. And Alkimidas won, was splendid. . . .
What else is life about? How else defy
what dogs us, day by day, gnawing our joints
with time's relentless teeth?

                          Gods have that knack,
but men can seem like gods in strength and speed
and deserve these hymns we sing of defiant praise.

5

Isthmia 5

From one altar red with blood to another red
with fire they run. It is cleansing but incomplete
until these words, like arrows of song, strike home
in the hearts of men, those citadels we assail
together with valor and talent.

                       Hours of training,
that discipline and pain, go mostly for nothing.
Runners, fighters, and charioteers all know
what losing is. And winning is sweeter than honey
in Zeus' cup. Phylakidas, having won
the wrestling-boxing combo, shows us the bloom
of life in the strength and skill of his hands and wits.
All Aigina rejoices; the world of men
exults in the demonstration: blood runs down
but the tongues of fire ascend, even to heaven.

A Garland for Meleager,
the Gadarene Swain

1

In my ear, a tinnitus of lust, and in my eye
a shimmer of body parts refracted by
tears of joy and desire. Both day and night—
and which is the more lubricious?—I am quite
undone by the wings of Eros, beating. They
carry the imp god hither, but never away.

5

Imagine souls as butterflies: they flirt
with the flames that fascinate though they do hurt.
Then ardor, or say the flame, having done its thing
will do as Eros always does—take wing.

7

What nights we've had, Kleobulos, of desire
so hot as to suggest the funeral pyre
of that last bed we face. O friend of mine,
upon my ashes pour unwatered wine:
my ghost may stagger down to Hades squiffed
and happy, Eros' witty little gift.

16

This wine
all by itself is fine,
but how much better
it can be when we wet our
lips with mead.
That honeyed wine, indeed,
suggests how it must be

when Kleobulos and he,
the young Alexis, do
whatever they do. Those two,
the man and that luscious lad,
are a sweetness one would add
to sweetness. How divine!
I toast them in honeyed wine.

22

Damned Dawn, why do you thus delay
the breaking of the day,
now that under Demo's cover
a new and loutish lover
fondles the pretty girl who was
my own once. Oh, it does
seem most unfair: then you would race
to roust me from that place
where each of us so well delighted
the other all night. It
is a plot—a joke you have enjoyed? a
case of *Schadenfreude!*

26

O Venus, who are
the morning star,
you take them away
but then you return
at the end of the day
again to burn
as the sky grows black
when you give them back,
and there you are
as the evening star
to shine again
on women and men.

27

Take her the message again and a third
time! Dorcas, a go-between
must be persistent. Send her word
of how I feel. Say what I mean.
Hurry, go. . . . No, wait. First try
your recitation out. . . . Or, no,
silence might work, for she knows I
have sent you. . . . With words? With presents? Go,
and look disheveled and desperate. Do
as I would do. With feeling say
what I would say. I'll go with you:
so you won't get lost, I'll lead the way.

33

Consider life and fate,
you who do great
deeds in the hope of glory that cannot die.

It is unfair, but funny,
that a pet bunny
can do as well—and I didn't even try.

In my sweet Phanion's lap,
I used to nap.
Snatched from my mother's breast, I nuzzled hers.

With her own hand she fed
me bits of bread
and the dainties from her plate a pet prefers

to proper rabbit food.
It's not a good
nutritional programme—and I grew fat,

with my belly overfilled.

Her kindness killed
her pet. In grief, she mourned: "Requiescat!"

And now my body lies
where her dear eyes
can see me from her bed. She dreams of me.

A hero's *kleos* I
have earned. And why?
The fates do not explain what they decree.

46

Heliodora's Whisper

Sweet Eros, I
should prefer to hear
in my inner ear
her gentle sigh
than the thrilling strum
all the gods admire
in their lofty home
of Apollo's own lyre.

50

From Heliodora, I flee, for I am not
a lunatic or stupid. I haven't forgot
those cataracts of rage and rivers of tears.
My marching orders are clear, but it appears
my soul is mutinous. Shameless and weak, it betrays
its duty and reason, and, knowing better, stays.

53

Tears again, more painful tears than ever before
    I give you, Heliodora, and as I weep,

I imagine these useless offerings trickling down to Hades,
        a tomb libation to which our love is now
distilled. A mere wraith of my former self, Meleager
        yearns for your ghost and sends it these love tokens.
Where is that perfect, delicate bud? Hades has snatched it
        away. Its blossom lies in the dust, befouled.
O mother Earth, I turn to you in my grief and implore,
        embrace her with that gentleness she deserves.

55

Walk softly, stranger, for in this place
        is an old man's grave: he sleeps
the long sleep all mortals face.
        Of the god of love, who weeps
such exquisite tears, this poet sang.
        He had the Muses' gift.
Eukrates' son, from Tyre he sprang,
        with its lovely boys. He left
for Gadara then that reared him, and Kos
        where he lived out his span
of years. If you are Syrian, thus:
        "Salaam." Or for the man
from Tyre, "Naidos." For the Greek,
        "Chaire." All hail! And you
may answer in whatever tongue you speak
        as decency prompts you to do.

Horace: Ode XXXVIII

That Chinoiserie, dear boy . . . I hate it!
And all that froufrou carving, acanthus leaves
and roses . . .
                    It's too mucking fuch!
                              A simple wreath
of good old-fashioned myrtle will suit me fine.
And a glass of chilled white wine out under the arbor,
with a competent servant waiting nearby to pour.

Blueprint for Disaster

by Christian Morgenstern

A river called the Snake,
unhappy about the lack of any sane ecological policy,
takes itself in hand one fine day
and ups and leaves.

A man called Tony,
watching it mosey along across the prairie,
whips his shooting iron out of his fancy holster
and ups and kills it.

The critter called the Snake,
is ashamed of itself and of what has now happened,
but too late, too late—the entire territory
ups and parches.

The man called Tony,
blowing the smoke from the end of his barrel,
hasn't the foggiest notion of what he has made happen.
Oops, it's dreadful!

The man called Tony,
unrepentant but nevertheless to some degree atoning
(the environment, after all, is all around us),
ups and croaks.

Summons (*Die Behörde*)

by Christian Morgenstern

Korf receives one day from the coppers
one of those B-9 forms, so-called because they aren't:
Who? Where? How? Why? And other such stumpers and stoppers.

Married? Single? Divorced? Separated? Other?
(Supply all relevant and requisite documentation
to support these claims.) *And the Maiden Name of your Mother?*

Visa? Permit de séjour? Papieren? Pass?
Credit rating? Or bluntly and plainly, are you a legitimate person
or are you perhaps no one? A nothing? A member even of the torturable class?

Failure to fill out the form will subject the subject
to penalties only some of which are specified hereinunder—
forfeitures, fines, confinement, etc. Signed, Oberuntergruppenführer Hecht.

Clearing his throat, with a discreet, "Korf!" he replies, "I insist,
on my right, notwithstanding any covenants and codicils to the contrary,
and as the party of the first part, to deny that I officially exist."

Agape, aghast, a-gasp, the deputy superintendent clutches at his chest in what
could be a coronary.

Like a Loony

A Traduction of Jack Leopard's "Alla Luna" by Larry Venuti,
Who Once Translated "Riso Bianco," Which Means "Boiled
Rice," as "With a Blank Smile"

O gracious loony, I remind myself
how, a vulgar year ago, with this sovereign collie,
I came in pain and agony to gaze at you:
You had hanged yourself in some forest,
sick or perhaps homosexual, and having risked everything.
Your mother was nebulous and tremulous as a painting
that surged from the ceiling before my eyes.
Your power appeared much the worse for having traveled.
That was my life too. (And it doesn't change its style, does it?)
O my mad dilettante! My coffee was black,
as I recall, and it renewed the estate
of my sadness. Oh, like a great occurrence
of the time of youth, when the anchor plunges
into the brief spume, the memory grows coarse.
The remembrance of past times like those
is an anchor of sadness, and the trouble of it endures.

Alla luna

O graziosa luna, io me rammento
Che, or volge l'anno, sovra questo colle
Io venia pien d'angoscia a rimirarti:
E tu pendevi allor su quella selva
Siccome or fai, che tutta la rischiari.
Ma nebuloso e tremulo dal pianto
Che mi sorgea sul ciglio, alle mie luci
Il tuo volto apparia, che travagliosa
Era mia vita: ed è, né cangia stile,
O mia diletta luna. E pur mi giova

La ricordanza, e il noverar l'etate
Del mio dolore. Oh come grato occorre
Nel tempo giovanil, quando ancor lungo
La speme e breve ha la memoria il corso,
Il rimembrar delle passate cose,
Ancor che triste, e che l'affanno duri!

—*Giacomo Leopardi*

Broads

Jorie

Then she came to the very edge of the room and looked down.
Below, a real commode gaped in its parts, white, white,
the two elements touching, water and air.
She thought of where the stomach opened out
and its sheer loss of intelligence,
the upsurging reflux of the drink in which a vulture now hung,
black in the foul depths of her acid and bile,
waiting, frozen, malevolent, until its moment's ripeness,
and the feathers of its wingtips touched the back of her throat
seeking an ending, seeking release. Until the laws of metabolism and digestion
    were repealed.
All of an instant, the properties were no longer knowable,
but what was there to understand? She let fly,
leaning outward over the edge as others had done before.
How close can two worlds get, the white and the clear
and then the dark and viscid and bitter, the rasping notes of a cello
into the thin air, and tears pouring down, wanting to die,
wanting to undo the entire evening, her soul
furious and ready to leave along with the Pepperidge Farm goldfish
and the fifth tequila sunrise
in its entirety?
What is it pulls at one, she wondered,
as she stared down into the mouth of the big white phone.
This has nothing to do with *telling the truth*,
this does not take *talent*.
Oh, it has its vibrancy, she was willing to admit,
an emptiness, an escape from the mind's
endless posturing and intellection.
Here at the edge of the toilet, she felt,
as if for the first time, how dismal it was to be an ordinary human being.

Sharon

Life is a bed and we are all sexual beings.
This fountain pen I caress with my hand pours forth
an endless ejaculate onto the paper, but I remember the
dipping pen I had in school, that first
poor skinny thing with its dear uncircumcised nib.
I had to keep putting it into my inkwell
every few words—another phrase and another
quick intromission. Writing poems is like that still.
The spidery letters are the telltale crust on my sheets,
and you, dear reader, are my mother, who did my laundry,
knowing what I'd been up to, but never saying a word, out
of kindness, or was it merely politeness?
I never knew. Anyway, we needed the money.

Lucie

I was lurking at the diagonal
Of your trapezium, humming

Mystical & possibly meaningless chants
I've sometimes overheard from the tipsy janitor

Mopping his way along these corridors,
The philosopher of Philosophy Hall

Electric with resentment, having caught
However undeservedly my basilisk notice.

Does he perhaps resent my radiant condescension
reckoning how much smarter I am than he is?

Or it is not that, but *obvious, external, and formal,*

his being bald as an egg & my having such lopecian endow-
ments,

A setic plenitude, a cultivated lavishness
Of hair, my vatic, numinous coiffure.

Louise
"Vetch"

Nobody knows the minor discomforts I've seen. . . .
You have no place in my garden,
your pinnately compound leaves terminate
in uninteresting tendrils,
and your variously colored flowers are all too drab.
I have had to walk a fair distance
to see you growing tediously at the edge
of this sunbaked meadow.
I come out here sometimes
to hear the plants and report
back what you tell me.
This is, I have believed,
the beginning of wisdom, the beginning of love.

But you have nothing whatever to say for yourself,
and it is very warm, and I am thirsty and I think
I am going home now.

Bette Davis: The Tragic Muse

Catharsis, Aristotle claims,
is that for which the tragic aims.
Pity and terror lead the way,
but at the ending of the play
with Oedipus blind, or Hamlet dead
and Lear, and the last sad couplet said,
we are purified and emptied who
have followed the action. This holds true
the other way, for when we've moved
our bowels we are likewise improved
and feel an enlargement of the soul on
such occasions, as the colon
shrinks to its former size and state.
Some, in the toilet, as they wait
on nature's call, elect to read,
but connoisseurs feel no such need,
who value ritual, for we
who delight in metaphor can see
the world in a little room. In this
repeated passionate synthesis
of mind and guts, we all come near
the resignation that King Lear
may feel the moment before he dies.
Delivered and relieved, we rise,
the frailties of flesh forgot.
As Bette Davis put it, "What
a dump!" She all but spat the line
in triumph—hers, and yours, and mine.

Remembering Marcello

"When I first come to America," he said
with only the slightest accent for which, nonetheless,
he smiled in rueful apology (or was that his habit,
the face he put on for the world for most occasions?)
"I know only the one word," he said, "fook"—
pronounced that way, a joke, but then on whom,
for the smile adjusted itself to the afterthought
a breath later, "but that word was enough."

Feet: An Anniversary Nonet

for Janet

We need for ourselves, my dear, a new figure,
something domestic, homely, and just a bit silly,
as, for example, my feet: the way that the one

can nestle into the other, the ball of the right
into the arch of the left, and the heel of the left
snug in the arch of the right. . . .
                                        I am not my feet,

but look down on them as God I hope looks on us,
happy that parts of his body go well together,
and, from how they conform and comport, taking some comfort.

Domitian at Ostia

When the sun glints bright
and the breeze is right,
      one is prompted then to go
and put out to sea
where the soul can run free
      at least for an hour or so.

When the day is clear,
one thrills to hear
      how the rigging snaps in the ship's
spars, while the stays
hum their hymns of praise.
      You can also hear the whips

as the galley slaves
dip their oars in the waves
      to the tunes the bosun sounds,
and our wake's white scud
is flecked with blood
      from their randomly crosshatched wounds.

Oh, it's splendid to ride
an outgoing tide,
      and the heart of a sailor soars
like a great seabird
for his having heard
      that rhythmic splash of the oars.

When the sun glints bright
and the breeze is right,
      one is prompted then to go
and put out to sea
where the soul can run free
      and sail for an hour or so.

Recent Acquisitions

Professor Dewberry Oldbury of the Newbery Library announces the following recent acquisitions:

The Mystery of the Charity of Charles Péguy by Geoffrey Hill
The History of the Mystery of Charles Chan by Earl Derr Biggers
The Mystery of the Comedy of Charles Chaplin by Charles Champlin
The Morbidity of the Calumny of Charles de Gaulle by Jean-Paul Sartre
The Monstrosity of the Chastity of Charles Bovary by Enid Starkie
The Catastrophe of the Mastectomy of Emma Bovary by Dr. Tim Johnson
The Quality of the Ministry of Billy Graham by Charles Colson
The Clarity of the Mendacity of Richard Nixon by John Dean
The Concinnity of the Misanthropy of Adolf Hitler by Martin Heidegger
The Grotesquerie of the Philosophy of Martin Heidegger by Harold Bloom
*The Complexity of the Colostomy of W. H. Auden: A Symposium on His
    "Letter to a Wound"*

Bucolic Lines Composed en Route to Lyon's U-Pik-'Em Strawberry Fields, Creedmore, N.C.

Let's all live somewhere in Creedmore,
where life is simpler. We need more
solitude. We'll prune and weed more,
go to nightclubs less. We'll read more,
drink Wild Turkey, go to seed more,
fool around a lot and breed more,
maybe slash our wrists and bleed more,
where good old boys have R.I.P.ed more
tranquilly out here in Creedmore
        than anywhere I know.
        It's calling us. Let's go!

Niagara Falls

Niagara Falls
delights, astonishes, appalls,
and then is boring. Still, people come, as if
there were something to be learned from watching vast quantities of water pour
over a cliff.

PS3569.L3

is how librarians think of me.
Once it was cute, but now it's chronic.
One even needs some neat mnemonic:
    A letter's addendum;
    the year of my birth;
    a lively perversion
    (for ribald mirth);
    L for the fifty books . . . And 3?
    The patriarchs of Jewry!
It spreads its way along the shelf
and is what I may someday call myself.